THE BIGGEST SECRET IN RETAILING

CHAOS TO CONTROL IN 30 DAYS

CHRIS MACKEY

Published 2020

Million Dollar Author

Million Dollar Author publishing
Sydney, Australia

Book Layout © 2020 Business Growth Advisors

The Biggest Secret in Retailing. -- 1st ed.
ISBN 978-0-6487202-1-8

Dedicated to all the amazing people I have attracted into my life. How could it possibly get better than this? Chris Mackey

Everyone has a plan until you are punched in the mouth

— MIKE TYSON

ABOUT THE AUTHOR

Retail Veteran & ActionCOACH Business Coach Chris Mackey is a retail veteran with more than forty years experience in senior management roles for a variety of Australia's leading businesses.

His expertise includes National Marketing and Promotion Manager for a top 50 ASX company; General Manager of Campbell's Cash and Carry; launching the IGA supermarket brand in Australia; and extensive international business operations training.

He now shares his wealth of knowledge to empower others to succeed in running their businesses. As an ActionCOACH business coach, he helps individuals recognize the value of their unique skills and to find creative solutions to their business challenges.

CONTENTS

NEW OPPORTUNITIES 1

YOUR TRADING STOCK IN THE NEXT 30 DAYS 5

THEFT IS ON THE RISE 11

SUPPLIER RELATIONSHIPS ARE A HIGHLY VALUABLE ASSET...15

Conflict Tactics...21

WHEN IS SOCIAL MEDIA TO MUCH? 27

ROSTER PLANNING..32

MANAGING CASH FLOW 36

HOW TO GET MORE HELP 40

CHAPTER ONE

NEW OPPORTUNITIES

13th March 2020, my whole world or the view of my world for the coming months changed, as I'm sure it has done for all of you.

My 60th birthday was only a couple of days away and I had been wondering how to make this milestone really memorable. Well, as it turned out, that decision was made for me - Australia shut down due to the coronavirus pandemic!

Fast forward to today and we are all now very entrenched into living in quarantine and isolation, with a whole heap of new social laws and interactions. Most businesses and certainly most food retailers are having to pivot into new directions and try to understand how the landscape is going to look for them.

I have put together this mini book in the hope that I can give you some tactics that will help you be creative and better able to capitalise on the opportunities that are available. By doing this, your retail food business will come out a lot better when this pandemic ends.

There is likely a fair bit of chaos in three main areas of your business right now. Through this book, I'm going to give you some tactics to deal with these areas and remind you of some of the basics in retailing.

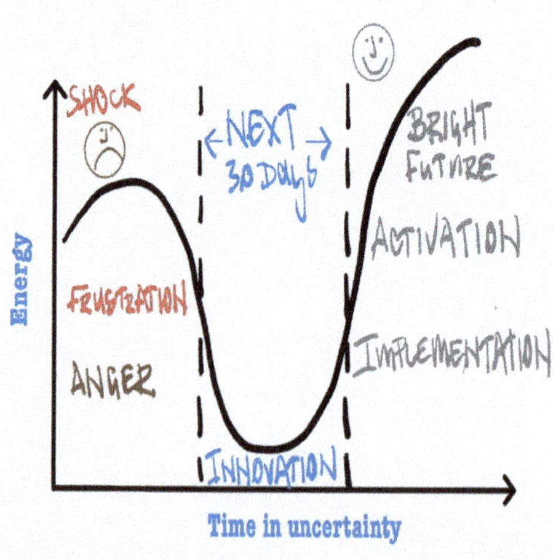

I've earned the right to write this book, not just because I've been in retailing and wholesaling for over 45 years - I was also the key person responsible for launching IGA Supermarkets in Australia. Now, as a business coach, I coach retailers all around the country on how to grow and prosper their businesses.

The Biggest Secret In Retailing is that by using your existing Skills, returning to some of the basics, and then getting creative, you can find new ways to thrive in the ever changing times we are in.

Let me show you how to use your skills to develop a plan for your operation that will help you overcome some of the challenges you are facing and to recognize new opportunities as they appear.

CHAPTER TWO

YOUR TRADING STOCK IN THE NEXT 30 DAYS

Supply of your trading stock is likely to be outstripping demand right now. Stock shortages will be the new normal for quite some time.

In this chapter, I want to talk to you about three areas of your retail food business:

- Buying from other sources.
- Buying local.
- The squeaky door gets the oil.

You can't sell stock that you don't have. In these times of stock shortages, the old saying "stack it high and watch it fly" just is not going to happen again for a very long time.

There are a couple of mindset changes that you need to embrace in the next 30 days. The first is about taking a risk on alternative suppliers from alternative markets or channels that you may not have considered before.

The other mindset that you need to challenge is the worry about damaging your supplier relationships.

Here are some tactics that you can use to improve your position on the stock in your retail food store:

#1. ASK SUPPLIERS FOR UPDATES REGULAR-ILY AND ASK VERY LOUDLY.

Why does your competition appear to have stock and you don't? It's because they are leveraging their buying power with their suppliers to give them some preferential treatment.

You've paid your suppliers regularly; you've behaved responsibly and ethically and now all you're asking for now is regular updates on supply positions.

What do they have available?

#2. BUYING LOCALLY PRODUCED AND SOURCED PRODUCTS.

If you have not already done so, review your inventory and identify what products are made and packaged here in Australia. If your business uses an automatic ordering system, consider putting a boost on Australian made and packaged.

#3. TALK WITH YOUR SUPPLIERS MORE AS PARTNERS, RATHER THAN DEMANDING THINGS FROM THEM.

A great lesson I learnt from mentors, was the squeaky door gets the oil. It's very accurate and it starts with your mindset.

If you expect to get preferential treatment from your suppliers, you have to be prepared to talk and collaborate.

So maybe you've got to work out that you can receive stock earlier in the day, or later in the day.

You can work out win-wins for everyone on deliveries. How can you help them? What about preferential payments? You're very cashflow positive in a retail food business right now.
Could you offer a quicker payment period in return for the stock? Unless you ask, you won't know if this is a possibility.

My objective with the above three tactics is to get you to thinking about what you need, what your must-have products in your business are and to list them.

How hungry are you to have those stock items? It's time to start exploring things that you've never done before. This is how we get around to breaking some of the rules.

What alternatives are out there? How much time are you actively spending this week thinking about alternate suppliers and other channels to source your products?

I recently saw on social media that an independent supermarket, unable to get supplied with household toilet rolls by their traditional wholesaler, had managed to source industrial-sized toilet rolls as an alternative. Now that is out of the box thinking!

One of my coach clients who has a top-end European delicatessen has offered to pay the freight to get stock to her business. This was enough incentive for the supplier to give her preferential treatment.

Click this link, or copy into your browser to watch an interview with Roz White on how her supermarkets have created a niche from supporting local products:

https://www.youtube.com/watch?v=uPXmX96JTGQ&t=9s

Your stock in the next 30 days

- [ ] Ask suppliers for updates regularly
- [ ] Buy locally produced and sourced
- [ ] Talk with your suppliers
- [ ] Communicate
- [ ] Follow up

It's never been truer that you can't sell what you don't have! So, break some rules, collaborate with your suppliers.

CHAPTER THREE

THEFT IS ON THE RISE

An old manager once taught me that if you treat people like criminals, then they can act like criminals.

However, theft is on the way up and if your trading stock is not monitored continuously, it's most likely on someone's radar for robbery. So, what can you do to reduce theft within your organisation?

My experience both in retailing and now, as a business coach, has shown me that regardless of what business it is, when the owner gets busy, the first thing that they stop doing is the basics.

The basics within your store security is something that you know you should be doing. However, because you are busy, perhaps you have stopped being so diligent with receiving stock - do you always check it all off? Now, I'm not suggesting that your suppliers are thieves. There is, however, an opportunity for some stock to get missed off the invoice. Unfortunately, some of your suppliers could be light-fingered at times. A drum of cooking oil, for example, that was invoiced to your business could be sold on the black market for a con-siderable amount of money, and when money is very tight, theft escalates.

What about internally? What about your check seal systems? All the staff know that when they make a purchase, they've got to get a check seal or some simi-lar style of approval. However, when you get busy does this fall by the wayside?

One of the most effective ways of deterring theft and increasing your store security is your physical presence on the shop floor. This is one of the very first things you discovered when you were learning the retail food business. Have you stopped this now that you are so busy?

Many businesses have gone to cashless which is a godsend but, if you are still dealing with cash, please be careful and diligent with all money handling.

So, remember, what got you here today won't get you there tomorrow if you have forgotten the basics, and that's what I hope you get out of this chapter.

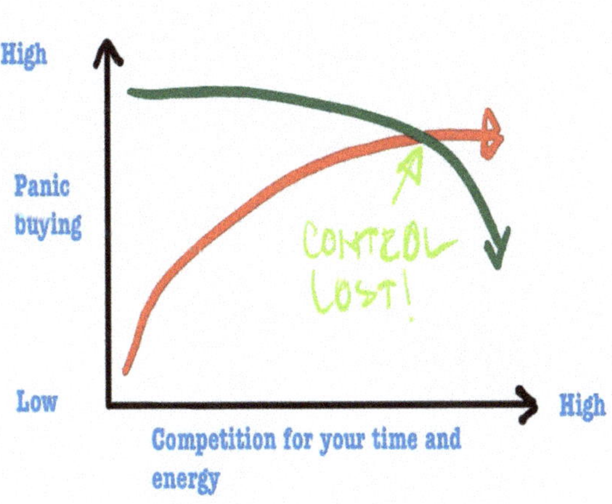

CHAPTER FOUR

SUPPLIER RELATIONSHIPS ARE A HIGHLY VALUABLE ASSET

In an ideal world, the relationships that you have built with your suppliers over the years are substantial. However, this is not always the case. Think about these relationships. Do you consider them to be critical to your business?

The job of your team is to look after your customers. That's not your job. Your customers' responsibility is to pay you for the goods and services that they receive. Your job is to pay your suppliers so that they can supply you with stock.

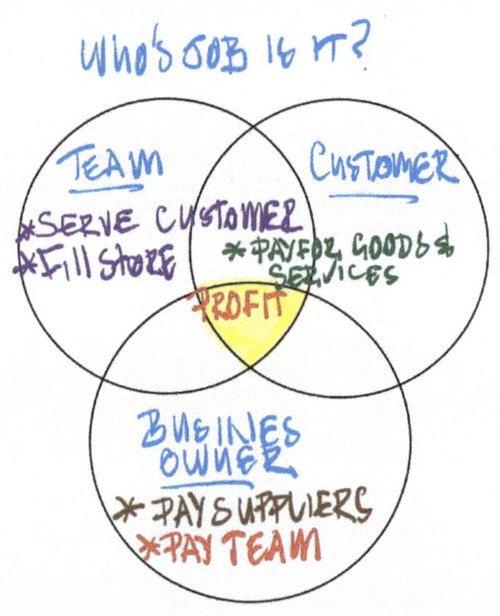

This is how the circle should operate. Often though, as the owner of the business, you think your job is to look after your team, your customers and your suppliers.

You are doing everything and that's what is so frustrating.

Let's look again at the role your suppliers play in your business.

What retailers are hoping they are going to get out of the amount of time and energy that they've invested in their supplier relationships is some preferential treatment during times like this pandemic crisis.

However, your supply of stock can now be inconsistent and that will add to any burdens and worries that you might already be carrying.

Suppliers are critical to your survival. Now is the time to shift your mindset 180 degrees when you are thinking about them because they also have wants and needs.

Here are some tactics that you can use today and over the next 30 days, to strengthen your relationships with your suppliers.

The first is to allocate some time in your day for these critical relationships. Think about how you can negotiate win-win situations. You will likely always have to give something in order to receive something.

What are your strengths right now? What are you able to offer your suppliers that positions you as a leader and someone that they want to do business with?

This is also a great time to inquire about returning surplus stock that you may have. If it's surplus to you, that doesn't mean that it's surplus to somebody else. Perhaps now is the time to approach your suppliers about returning this surplus. The answer just might be "yes".

During my career, I've worked as a buyer for two of the major supermarket chains. There were stock shortages time to time, for various reasons, though certainly not as dramatic as we have now. During these times, the industry would go onto stock allocations.

What that meant was that if Coles and Woolworths were 80% of the marketplace, then they got 80% of the stock.

Sounds fair and logical, however, as a buyer for an independent supermarket chain that wasn't going to get preferential treatment because of our market share, I had to form compelling arguments with our suppliers as to why we needed it. This is where some creative thinking and negotiating comes in.

Generally Coles or Woolworths retail outlets receive a delivery every day from their warehouse, whereas an independent supermarket in some instances may only get a delivery once a week. This means that Coles and Woolworths might be out of stock of an item for a day or two, but an independent supermarket might have to wait a fortnight.

By negotiating with your suppliers, you may be able to find a different way to get preferential treatment - perhaps by ordering on a particular day of the week or ordering in a specific configuration of full trucks or full pallets. Maybe your argument instead will be that because you don't get a daily delivery, you need some preferential treatment.

CHAPTER FIVE

CONFLICT TACTICS

The new rules about social interactions are in place now. It's not something that you, as a food retailer have decided to do - it's the law. However, there are still different interpretations of these rules that are catching many food retailers unaware.

Customers are just as confused, if not more so, than your team. The rules seem to be constantly changing, taking away more and more of the freedoms we have all taken for granted. Grocery shopping has become very stressful and time consuming. It's no wonder people are angry and frustrated.

In this pandemic reality of stock shortages and long line ups that we are living in right now, you and your team may not always be shown the respect you deserve from your customers and from the community.

You have invested much time, energy, and money in your organisation and now your frontline team is having to sometimes deal with your customers' anger and frustration, and in some cases, abuse. Perhaps they are taking more time off for stress, or even worse, resigning and finding employment in other areas, or just taking up some of the government grants that are available to them.

I don't think there has ever been a better time to give your team extra training in communication and conflict management skills. This will give them tools that they likely need on a daily basis right now.

Here are some tactics your team can use to help reduce conflict:

1. Allow customers to talk

Allow angry customers to talk and express their feelings until they release their frustration and calm down.

2. Show you care

Use empathy statements to show you understand the customer's feelings or frustrations.

3. Use the correct tone

Don't smile, laugh or mock upset customers. Convey empathy with a soft tone.

4. Be neutral

Do not offer your opinion, agree or disagree with customers. Offer empathetic support and work to solve their problems effectively.

5. Don't react

Never respond to angry comments. Allow the customer to voice their opinion and interject with helpful redirection when appropriate.

6. Focus

When a customer is on a tangent, redirect the conversation back to the important issues and focus his attention on constructive solutions.

7. Use verbal softeners

Use words like "likely", "typically", "perhaps", "sometime", "possibly" or "occasionally" with customers who might not respond well to categorical words like "always" or "never".

8. Make angry conversations private

Avoid talking with angry customers within earshot of employees or other customers.

9. Agree

Find something to agree with the customer about. An agreement will result in collaboration and cooperation.

10. Use silences

When customers talk, listen and wait for a silence. When your customer has stopped talking, then summarize their main point and work together on a solution.

11. Use timeouts

If customers are frustrated, annoyed, or are not capable of engaging in a productive conversation, allow them the opportunity to think by themselves for short periods of time. Then, address their concerns effectively.

12. Set limits

When customers refuse to act constructively and alternative methods have been exhausted, set limits and end the interaction.

Learning how to avoid conflict whenever possible is always the best tactic. If a conflict is already in progress, then knowing how to diffuse it quickly is a very valuable skill to have.

You could also do something really out of the box. Spend 30 minutes once a week asking some of your customers for feedback on how you could improve their experience as they leave your premises. This would certainly get you ahead of the curve in the whole retailing situation right now.

And if you still are finding that your team is copping abuse, think of employing a security guard as a last resort.

These are fundamental things, but often you think that your team should know this, but they don't. They've never experienced situations like we're in right now.

CHAPTER SIX

WHEN IS SOCIAL MEDIA TO MUCH?

"How often should your business be doing social media posts?" is a question that is frequently asked by retailers.

I believe there is no right or wrong answer to this. I think the key is more about offering value, rather than just volume.

There is a saying that you can't bank Facebook likes and that's so true.

Often times you know your business should be using social media more often, but you don't. The number one reason for most is a fear of haters and nasty comments that can happen for Facebook users.

However, there has never been a better time to use Facebook to create new ways to stay in touch with your customers.

It's a way for you to be able to show leadership and to have a calming influence within your community. It's also something that can be measured, whereas radio advertising and catalogue advertising is not measured at all.

60% of the country use Facebook regularly and 50% use Facebook daily, according to socialmedia.com.au.

So, your customers are active on Facebook, and if you're not, you will not able to speak to them in real-time.

I want to share three tactics with you that you can use right now that will get you better results over the next 30 days.

1. Start a Facebook group for your business and get as many of your customers as possible to join it.
This is a very cost-effective communication tool that allows you to communicate directly to your customers in a personal way. It's a free feature of Facebook groups and it's the modern equivalent of a database or CRM system.

Customers will get to know you, the owner, significantly better and you can share as much or as little of your personal life as you like.

#2. If you are doing your own Facebook posts already, consider giving this job to one of your team members. If you can pay somebody $18 an hour to do these for you, it's a lot better use of your time.

#3. Plan what you're putting out on Facebook and do a minimum of three posts per day.

Your job will be a lot more effective if the goal is to fix your customers' pain points. Offer value, versus volume. One efficient thing you could do is let people know when deliveries have arrived. Pretty simple, isn't it. But the pain for your customers is that they never know when you're fully stocked. By letting the community know that your delivery has arrived and that it will be on the shelves in two hours, pain fixed.

You can make specific offers to your customers and also give them a prior warning that, FYI, toilet rolls have just turned up, or that carrots are just in.

If you are always striving to solve someone's problems, you can never get it wrong.

Your business is going to springboard out of the pandemic better than you came in.

ASSIGN TASK
PLAN CONTENT
SHOW LEADERSHIP
START FB GROUP

CHAPTER SEVEN

ROSTER PLANNING

I think we would all like to have things go back to the way they were before this pandemic.

We don't even know what our new normal is going to be when it is all finished. However, I am quite sure it's not going to be the same as it used to be.

Right now, labour costs are rising. Customers' shopping habits have changed so much that it is very difficult to gauge the demand for checkout staff. Delivery times from your wholesalers have also become inconsistent.

In all of this, you want to be able to sustain the increases in your cost of doing business.

Three reasons I think you need to look at rosters:

1. Rosters give you flexibility.

2. Rosters can rein in some of the cost increases that you're incurring.

3. Rosters can help you to look after your customers, because ultimately if you're not doing that, then nothing else matters.

Do you remember the five Ps?
Proper
Planning
Prevents
Poor
Performance.

It's a management tool that has been around for years, and I think it's going to serve you well right now.

So, here's a 30-day roster challenge for you that will help you manage your wage percentage:

Make sure that you continue to get your departments to schedule their labour and present it to you, even though you are busy.

Immediately get your teams into a WhatsApp group. It's a free social media platform. If you don't already know about it, check it out on YouTube.

You can put all of your team into your WhatsApp group so that you can communicate instantly to either individuals or organisations. Use this valuable tool to give you the flexibility to quickly create or change rosters, by the hour, if necessary.

The Australian Fair Work Commission website goes into detailed explanations as to how you are now able to enter into more flexible arrangements with your casuals than ever before.

Most of us have had some experience in managing through disruptions and strikes, but nothing has been as long-lasting as this Coronavirus pandemic.

Don't stop roster planning because you're busy.

Busy is not a badge of honour and telling yourself that you're "busy" is preventing you from seeing a way forward.

CHAPTER EIGHT

MANAGING CASH FLOW

Even the most profitable business can still fail by running out of cash.

How often have you said to yourself "When it comes to managing cash flow, my accountant looks after that for me". Or "I'm not good at that financial stuff". What can you do today to keep cash in your business?

Often lack of knowledge creates fear of what the reporting is telling you about the health of your business and its cash flow.

There has never been a better time, in my opinion, to acquaint yourself with this critical piece of your business. Right now, your accountant is likely very busy and will not always be able to answer your questions in a timely manner. Therefore, the best thing you can do right now is to learn. Knowledge is power.

I have retail customers in my coaching practice that tell me they would rather drink a cup of urine than up skill themselves in their financial management! As funny as this sounds, it does illustrate how many people belief that it will be a next to impossible task.

However, there are things that you can do over the next 30 days that are easy to implement and that can make a significant difference.

Let's start:

1. Government Grants. Make sure that you're applying for the Grants that your business is qualified to receive. I've met business owners that are entitled to Grants who have not asked. However, these can certainly help with your cash flow.

2. Pay your bills on the date that they are due, not the date that your office manager chooses to pay them. As an example of that, I know a business where all invoices are paid on a Monday, even though they might not be due for another week or another fortnight.

By paying invoices on their due date, you are able to hold onto your cash for much longer.

3. Ask your major creditors for extended payments. If the answer is no, then ask if you can pay with a credit card, if you are not doing this already.

4. Who owes you money and how many days are they overdue? Apply the squeaky door gets the oil treatment and ring that person. If they can't pay immediately then offer to accept a credit card if you are not doing so already. Even if it means that you have to pay a merchant fee of 1.75%, you are still far better off having the cash in your account.

Cash is king!

LESS STRESS
PEACE OF MIND
EXTERNAL
INTERNAL
USE A CREDIT CARD
KNOWLEDGE IS POWER.
#1. GRANTS
Apply TODAY
#2 PAY INVOICES DATE DUE
HOLD ON TO CASH
#3 ASK MORE TERMS
WILL NOT BE OFFERED
#4. KNOW YOUR RECEIVABLE DAYS
CASH IS KING.

FINAL CHAPTER

HOW TO GET MORE HELP

We are continuing to develop coaching programs to guide retailers in all areas of growing their business past the next 30 days and spring from the reset we have just had into a new world in retailing.

If you want guidance, this is where you can get it: Connect with us on Facebook at https://www.facebook.com/Mackeybizcoach

Or join our private Facebook group for up to date guidance and tactics on the five ways to grow your business

https://www.facebook.com/groups/Bizgroup5ways

Or follow us on LinkedIn

https://www.linkedin.com/in/action-coachchrismackey/

Or visit our website

https://chrismackey.actioncoach.com/

Or Call Chris Mackey: 0437474556